Loveliest Grotesque

winner of the KORE PRESS FIRST BOOK AWARD

selected by Marilyn Chin

Loveliest Grotesque

Sandra Lim

KORE PRESS   Tucson

Kore Press, Inc.
PO Box 3044 Tucson, Arizona 85702

ISBN-13 978-1-888553-20-8
ISBN-10 1-888553-20-0

Designed by Lisa Bowden

Photograph by Valerie Galloway

www.korepress.org

PREVIOUS FIRST BOOK AWARD WINNERS: Jennifer Barber for *Rigging the Wind*,
selected by Jane Miller; Deborah Fries for *Various Modes of Departure*, selected by
Carolyn Forché; Elline Lipkin for *The Errant Thread*, selected by Eavan Boland.

We express our deep gratitude to those who helped make this Kore Press First
Book Award possible: The Tucson Pima Arts Council, The Arizona Commission
on the Arts, through appropriations from the Arizona State Legislature and the
National Endowment for the Arts, the manuscript readers, the judge, and all the
writers who submitted their work.

Contents

for my parents

No sadness, just disaster.

—Jasper Johns

Something Something Something Grand

Loveliest Grotesque

I kept the little ruin near me, I stowed it in the kitchen,
it sat in the pantry, like a jar of reddest jam,
it sang me songs of seafaring, it said the "weather being fine,"
I listened to it breathe, shiver brokenly in time,
I believed a multitude stood between us, four seasons,
the meaningless physical world, and a grammar primer,
you could see how I found it necessary,
with its immodest appeals, its constant state of *déshabillé,*
it is small for its age, it is too wide-awake,
so my sewing came undone with the years,
I stalked myself to the open door, the unlatched gate,
ma petite is a world sold of charms, it loves a new act,
has a leer for a mouth, has indecorous energy,
I ran from the spring glee of it, I radioed ahead,
oh I unplanned a lifetime, turned my gaze to the west,
but then it said it would make something of us both,
the sound of it touched me, fat in its cracked sadness,
it was homemade all along, it was oddly necessary,
I looked back like Lot's wife, like the exhausted mirage
that I was, and the loveliest salt taste was whelming us,
both awash in a light of knives, and the wind it was shifting like this—

Curious This

Sinister to meet you.
—

AM-ed in the new, true
wheels of heat, rings around
the town called rain.
Curious this.

It's a lark to be awake,
open-eyed, petals peeling,
hey . . . hey You.

       But the kitchen!
The coffeepot preens on the stove.
Fork tines are tuning,
tuning are the stainless-steel
glints. Mischievous. But they
ain't gonna tell.
Curious this.

Depression before spring? (Spring)?
Renewal is real new, but
goddamn, not a new real—

Cup and saucer gambol together,
I think
(er, is it your hands then, or nerves? (Nerves))?

In Radiant Serenity

I pound the steaks,
        you verb the noun.
I man the pipes,
        you still verb the noun.
I kill a bottle of wine,
        hawk the goods,
and work the ellipsis.
        You verb (like a smirk).
I verb you; you verb and verb.
        (Parenthetical remark).
There's an urgency growing
        on the set. To the tune of
adverb noun prepositional phrase,
        we position ourselves.

The Horse and Its Rider

tell me how to separate it / stasis from motion /

from ankle to earlobe / tall good-looking not very truthful / the surround asphalt
paths and thieves / strange turns of speech /

from shame I have paid attention / weak and dour and in thrall / scent of hot iron
on a shirt collar / "you with such fine legs" / blinkered reductions /

a city story / the furred expansiveness, natural chic / money / lovelorn, frantic / is
she or he the carrier or receiver of plagues? /

destiny as a craning question mark / a snob and a Marxist / freezing in a thin red
coat / all the bones lit up /

someone who belongs to another / what difference does it make to be here alone?
/ take this street, take this hand / eros has a thousand envoys /

now / now / wait for all the arrows to hit their mark / now / now I am going to be
happy / conditional / hardly birthright / strange, worn, contented dolls /

the *piano nobile* / an endless pageantry / now / let you be lifted / as a frost, old age
will take us /

cleave then / which way

Zealous

The baker curls the sugar off the ache.
My spot, bit hot and thunderpealed. You,
Clocked so quick to tender, my *pot-au-feu,*
My Lucky Strike. I was very hungry.
Outside, we've gone missing for days on end.
Push and pull, so keyed. How we keep the time.
The painter loves an uneven splendor.
Looking begs for action; we share the bite.
So intricate with pandemonium:
The magnolia as Arctic moonlight,
Chiaroscuro as annotation.
Dark-syllabled, the ABC of it,
My blush spreading its hands as if to say,
Unjoint and traveled, how certain you fit.
As it arrived I saw that it was spring.

Vexed Pressed Frock

around the ill na na we played jacks. hopscotch. swilled it to the tick-tack-toe. little
cosmonauts, blooming super-fools. crowing "ill na na" in the marmalade. told it
fortunes, explained the circulatory system. sassed it, na na, cheered madly madly.
gamely irritable, adorable. indolent and homemade. country mouse meet city mouse.
so glad like a birthday cake, ill na na.

And She Addressed the Ages and She Sighed

The truly foreign makes its case like one long telling kiss,
And finally the puzzling slows as mystery moves like this.
It thinks you over, unscrolls deeds, and coaxes time ahead,
The clocks admit their artifice as gracious tastes are fed.

Outside the dark apartment day had quickly climbed ashore,
And having made the fruit you said "I always eat the core."
Invisible is the whole of earth when standing on the edge,
That moss survives the fragile blooms cuts lovers' every pledge.

I wrung you from the lonely paths, I cut the rind and knew
The soul is neither raw nor vast but hewn and followed through.
What comes on like a language and is dreamed before performed
Hides deep and idle living, thick and heavily adorned.

Love and honor to the shameless thief, the bird that lights nowhere,
Each drop of darkness blushes, reinvents the winter air.
Outmoded, haughty, lost to gods, she drifts along the quays,
And now the mirror spins the hours and nothing native stays.

Three Fleas

the flea

seeks farther than the distance a beautiful wicked grin is going to answer you
follows the blood that starts in the missal and alights on the tip of the tongue
idiotic with travel he laughs as he's crushed salt to salt pluck and dive names sweet
as cakes Celias Julias Corinnas a little dog is always in the corner the smirk will
crest to ardor artichoke blooms dressmakers pins slipping songs pouring off their
wings and after what dies tiny stitches furiously ticking so it wins its freedom from
deepest exuberance tilted into the innocence of a number copying a life gently
now the nets part and run open and what did the poet say standing there in the
torn rows a waterfall widening happiness

the flea

squats in me beautiful crooner more human more doggy dealing heat here and
there little heaps of sugar the mottled peelings of pears massages the blood from
congestion introduces the Mexican border suture ligature my fan of bones won't
have it any longer arms akimbo dirty girl it soars up from the mincing hooves of a
pony the horsefly with satiny eyes dots the way decadent and needful in a state
library in the warm core of a split tree in the eagle-haunted passes milk chocolate
cigarette papers and after what dies the luxurious convalescence squandering joy
the carnage of august what does it matter hopes are high wink over a gorgeous
little casket someday arousing my whimsical greed

the flea

tells me the dream clots like blood upon waking but to be true stay true

Reasoning in a Raw Wind

Before you go
with the bullet bird—

what will you be looking
for?

        It was a Sunday,
and the old revolts opened

their tin trunks, dividing and
unmending us.

I wanted an old grotto, warm jewels,
and rotted teeth.

        —What was your wish?

That love would
hatch us

        whole and vertical.

        Amputations and erotics could
turn their seven sides.

Under a breaking surface, there
was

        true phosphorescence,
spiking the body

as it kept losing its place.

If you can
both go and observe—

glimpse blood tides, sample metal

you'd stand (a passage)

beside yourself, gone
and listening.

A Village Journal

Sun claw, coffee. Outside, a light sugary rain. Inside, a wet hem, smudged eyes. Roil of hips and then you taste it: memory shimmer, tin. Huge paws breaking the sky open, there once was so much sweetness, raw as wish, conditionless. No rush to it. A radiance hit your skin, but you mistook it. Now, as sheer as your secrets, you float in a low-flame rage. A technical rose.

Covers and uncovers you. Recollect, succulent, a generous cut. Slept with Robbie right away, so did Rosemary. Maybe too much night reading. Rose was ideal pornography, tumbling through supermarkets at night, sandwiches and cigarettes in her pockets. Stitches coming open, a fresh necklace. Muscle, tweed, silk. The season drew in its breath. And there was the ruthless cool of fluorescent lights, hoarfrost coating our blurred loveliness. I stayed. I was bitten. I could not make it down the block. He's thrown himself off the roof by now.

Riches in a different weather. We are trading notes through the grillwork. Or I alone am leaving these bright animal clamberings lying around. Each stare, a socket. I remember. Longing in the hot dark, a low crouching disturbing my green Aprils. Rebecca bent in half by love and wandering. Born in the desert, altogether water current. Lapping. She lived in the building with perpetually dark windows, a seam of unlit roses. Outside, a heat haze. Jumped with no wings.

Uncomely juvenilia. A procession of cold data fed like a wick through sleep. Skeletal and smuggled. The birds are stuttering. I cannot describe the joy of knowing that Ethan continues, more or less. He wants to delight. Sometimes the terror just breaks off: storms pass over the houses while inside, long warm winds roll over a quieted body. Remember the concert went on and on. That music was phantom pain compared to the red dog snapping at Leslie's great store. I am astonished by her. This is the movement that confused me then and now: disgust taking bites out of blitheness. Heavy as cowbells.

Staying on in a low land. Here I sit with my ham radio, hands folded. Lola says each love is by proxy. Adam writes me monthly, ends every letter with "do you know *this* horror?" What could you alter, come to this. Stay mid and swift. Recall is best and worst. And now carved from hunger, can't say that I am a *woman*. Can't say that it isn't excellent at times. Fall shudders red and ochre, clean through to a various pain. Sparkling. Outside, a graphic error (as you marry or lean forward in the passenger's seat or cough to cover your shame). Once, inside a night of live stars and other improbable skylights, the conversation seemed indispensable. I'll be so willing. Ever was. Ordinary behavior, and you can walk there.

Last Mash Note

Underneath the pews we gossiped and napped.
We sexed each other. Valuable information.

I took my philosophy in the parking lot.
Rolled around in the VW van, ill with learning.

After the books were returned to the library
we sat on our hands, our banners all aflutter.

I kept everything I liked: The shapes and
the smokes, and the partly bitten body.

I wanted to see the themes grow inside us
like a talent or a tumor. Pure accident.

We wake up in the middle of the night:
Ah—narcotic fragrance of burning ink—this is romance!

Night Lights

I walk towards the forest and a clandestine deformation starts to grow, as silent as a swan. The earth gives up a cold mist as my coughs break into tiny yellow birds soaring strong and high above me. They've hatched a sorceress, polished off the rough edges, turned on the night lights. The goat-footed boys walk all the way to me with bouquets of bees' wings as they beckon me to the boat. They hoof about with all the eager cheerfulness of a church social. The camel-eyed naiads alternately flutter and smolder by the edge of the lake, trying to lasso their glances around the boys' necks. Love is sweet here, a cowboy's vision of a pure ballerina. The water smells bitter and aromatic, and I could drift forever, until I meet the heavy gazes of the cygnets, who have been here all along. Their eyes are ringed with a swarthy blue huntedness, and I realize the lake is catching fire.

Of the Inconsistency of Our Actions

X points to a bruise. *Look*
at me.

And now,
something is hiving within.

You turn to X
like a big thought,

like an offer of all immoderacy.
So this is the new world.

X says seeing is believing. You think
on counter-illuminations. Seeing being innocence.

You stick your fingers where your eyes
used to be.

Sonnet

Red is the color but
Green holds the mood and
Black is the outstretched hand.

Grey is the uniform
While Pink keeps the dream
Yet Brown's the dominant theme.

Things get complicated:
Orange starts on cue,
Then Lemon Yellow, Prussian Blue.

How I sink into White and
Weep for Magenta,
Cling to Silver but

Eye Ultramarine.
Prickly Rose, I go to glean.

Something Something Something Grand

I adore you: you're a harrowing event.
I like you very ugly, condensed to one
deep green pang. You cannot ask the simplest
question, your hold is all clutch and sinker.
                              Cannibal old me,
with my heart up my throat, blasting on all sides
with my hundred red states. Hidden little striver.
How not to know it, the waist-deep trance of you,
the cursing, coursing say of you. Embarrassing today.
                              Curiouser and curiouser,
your body is a mouth, is a night of travel, your body
is tripling the sideways insouciance. The muscle
in you knows gorgeous, in you knows tornadoes.
In an instant's compass, your blood flees you like a cry.
                              You put on my heat,
(that's the way you work) I'm a bandit gripping
hard on the steal. The substitutions come swiftly,
hungering down the valley, no one question to cover
all of living. I arrange myself in the order of my use.
                              You're wrong and right
at the same time, a breathless deluxe and a devouring
chopping down the back door. You slap my attention
all over the dark. What's in me like a chime?
Sometimes, sometimes, I come to you for the surprise.

Ballad of the Last Chance

Occidental Fade In

Gradually, *lieux* became *milieux*. A small map showing only boundary contours without names. Reckless colors here and there, splashy, promising, & yet, I suspected a substrate of disappointment (of which the recurring motifs of faded wall-to-wall carpets and trips to the All Cardboard Zoo may be two, still extant, expressions. Why were there manatees at all?) At fourteen, Kafka not yet in the picture, I was accidentally exposed to *A Woman Under the Influence*. Secret, sleepy matinee. Then wandering out into the late afternoon sun, laying to rest vague but expectant dreams of the puma and the gnu—that wildebeest. Followed by the arch lighting up of one lovely, shaking, *meaningful* cigarette. Later, underscored by its smallness and separateness, this gesture projected as perverse *tour-de-force*. (At the time, I can admit it now, I was more involved in experiencing a lion's share of ecstasy & madness than in "being myself" or doing a job.) Thereafter, in thrall to dreamy lianas of every stripe, such baubles and Babylons, in boroughs, in hamlets, in the odd window dresser's barmy bender, through a long road trip across some forty-eight states and a trip to the old country (I went outside the lines again), a return to speed: wall-to-wall; estranged adjacency; renters in urban apartments. A homecoming as compelling as any other. (Minor diorama: a matchbox videotape next to a postage stamp stack of *The Complete Stories, Letters, The Diaries*. A diminutive Rand-McNally globe. The smallest stuffed giraffe.) In such nearness, nothing neighbors.

Ballad of the Last Chance

A mocking bird opens it: Prefix, suffix.
                              Out of sure futures, a voice embroiders.

Satie on the radio: Electric lights on dark waters.
                              Not a hibiscus blossom in sight.

It's an artificial, modern season: Flexible torsos,
                              négritude its own perfume,
                                             men biting into their paintings.

The apartment cats: Friendly, maybe pregnant.
                              All the upstairs intellectuals: On their knees for love.

The queen in the bar.
                    X writes plays (short): Forlorn purple mimeographs.

Here comes the gang of attractive *mal-aimés:* Sulky neatness in mordant colors.

       Nature: Lived as a value.

We grow dropsical: Crammed-head.
                              Everything cresting,
                                             nothing doing.

The scales and speed of odd juxtaposition: The song so fine and cold.

City heart, original food.
                    Survival & reverie salt the palate: Blue, blue fluorescence.

       A little Europe of tenements: Unfold the tiny flowers.

"The rhyme is the fire from building to building": The children chord up and down.

Lines spinning forth: Each swing out-winters the ice.

Time contracted, a concertina.
Let it have the strength of a crime: This endless task of transfer . . .

All you cannot help but conjure.
As the path of a spine: Indifferent and sure.

What it felt like: Summoned to the party.
Out of a past (a tilt, a roundelay): Seized into the make.

A mapping of enchantment—somatic, nearly wordless, & free.

Dishonestly true.

Break into the first blow: Even though all other parts of life are pulling you away.

The Red Smile

It is The Red Smile at table six in a breakfast room in Seoul.

Before long: Empires and expansions and the buried pulse of cause and consequence making its rounds.

For now, she does not know that she is The Red Smile, does not see beyond the cooling tea, the plastic carnations on the table, the thought of a dash across continents itching her feet.

The radio says, Goodbye and Hello. A song has passed into the language she knows, but it passes odd and scampering, like a broken horse.

She might never know that she's The Red Smile, the one with a genius for repetition, the one who, even blindfolded, finds the lungs of the city. We hold this moment, as much as we can grasp.

Her fingers half-curled around the white cup, she is thinking of her daddy, of the half-finished painting, of freckled flesh in other countries, of tiny fishing boats, and of the angles of flowers underwater. Here goes, she thinks, *here goes*. Time is ridiculous.

We must be pen pals, recognizing each other by distance, the squirm on our tongues or the prickles on our phantom limbs. We have so much energy and many more cities than that.

Where Metaphorical Moves Get Started

"The Red Smile," 1963. What were my parents doing then? They weren't thinking about Alex Katz, abstraction and figuration, illustration versus art. Nevertheless, in a speculative spirit, here is an instance of a world being made. Everything is already contemporary.

What have I to do with Ada or she to do with me? It is a cloudless red day with a steady stab of mellotron and a shake of the tambourine. Life is flatly painted, dramatically cropped. The oversized head recalls the movies and billboards. Where you might go for love, history, firepower. The first attraction was the risk she ran of romance or "mere" prettiness. Then perhaps it was the monumental scale, the cool detachment in that, and then the face working as interior and landscape.

—sub-rosa ways of understanding self and others. The blue streak you take as a personal asterisk.

Mother, me, Ada. Is it a work of persuasion? The moment is so airless and the decorative red smile burns off a human world. What makes the heart stop and form a vantage point is the realm she and red propose: your imagining must take on its own consistency. The ornamental lack of intimacy became somehow passionate and regretful. What is it here that hatched the abstract pleasure of me? The idiom of a culture, not a grammar of objects or perceptions. In the process of learning its shorthand, antinomies, and blank spots, the first improvised forms of contrary dreaming come to light.

What Is an Image?

That winter was filled with Kurosawa, iconology, and glossy French paperbacks. Our leader Alice was crisply made, dashing, shaped along the lines of a flute vase. In her glittering black eyes flickered Baudelaire's words, "Time eats life." Nick was trying to quit smoking by playing tennis and reading Lope de Vega. Miranda was our English, English rose who linked everything to *Sunset Boulevard* and tied up Billy Wilder in her coppery red hair. Marlo was sick the whole time: a pretty, drooping violet who dug in her heels each time we made a diagram about narrative desire. Desire! We ate it up and licked the spoon. We heard it in Fischer-Dieskau's sonorous voice, peered at it in the toe work of Maria Tallchief, felt it hot and cold in *Throne of Blood*. The kumquat trees outside made the days seem festive. Through the difficult rainy spells I stared at them and dreamt of kitchens: small kitchens with two burner stoves and hot plates plugged into peeling walls; immense kitchens with double-boilers, heavy oak tables, and tea tins scattered on window sills; the kitchens of summer homes: mismatched flatware, pineapple-shaped cutting boards, coffee percolators; restaurant kitchens with stainless steel for miles, mixing vats, and not a whiff of the intimacy of say, a hand garlic press; single persons' kitchens with cans of catfood, a lone Spanish onion, and an unwrapped Sunday morning paper. There was a wayward, carnal atmosphere in any kitchen. No longer a listener now, the daydreamer was winding through pages of corridors. The very last time I returned from my prowls, Eisenstein's lion was rising majestically in the twilight, Alice was quoting Wittgenstein's imperative to "Give up literary criticism!" and the thickening allusions alighted on all our shoulders with a look of loneliness.

Pantoum

Taking on an aspect of the Orient,
Skies full of hatchets and oranges
Love, uninvited, hangs in the blood:
But what is a kingdom to a dying emperor?

Skies full of hatchets and oranges
Keep the birds singing, sorrows fresh—
But what is a kingdom to a dying emperor,
As the nights grow steadily into mountains.

Keep the birds singing, sorrows fresh—
The princess braids these into a necklace
As the nights grow steadily into mountains,
Why, even regrets recede unexpectedly.

The princess braids these into a necklace:
Roads and rivers that lead away from the palace.
Why, even regrets recede unexpectedly
In a solitude full of wars and songs.

Roads and rivers that lead away from the palace
Never converge in that vast landscape;
In a solitude full of wars and songs,
The words remain light and fugitive.

Never converge in that vast landscape
In the way that stars keep their distance.
The words remain light and fugitive
In an anticipation crossed with absence.

In the way that stars keep their distance,
Love, uninvited, hangs in the blood
In an anticipation crossed with absence,
Taking on an aspect of the Orient.

Measure

Girls

              For the lowing of whales
has conjured them up   given them savage details,
cut off their braids.   Seahorses ride their eyes
out. I am one of those   with a dimple in the mind.
A gleam in the foam   astral, tonight. Don't ruin
them with—   don't wake them, the warm
anemones deflate it.   Failing sun, go after
sand, all thousand bits.   Ocean me, be larger than
promise. Eased into skirt.   Talk not of mermaids.

Whales

              The vaulting green and drift
of that day   white distances opened, run high.
Blue proceeds   —like bones, like time— to
its designated junctures,   tremendous as girls.

Bovary in the Late Afternoon

The part where she buys the poison and dies is very true.

———

That you should be thinking of Emma now,
or rather not her, but the white frock
and the pooling bit of black blood at her collar.
Pretty puss, stocked like so much berry preserve
in a pantry full of domestic grotesqueries.

That you read the wrong books (they murmur),
or simply that no one appreciated (like you, *chérie)*
how bewitching and intimate a yellow silk
ottoman could be.
                      Scarlatina, consumption, the gout.
No *l'action, l'amour* there. Was it just
that Charles never allowed you an entire day
to pick out a pastry, smoke in your bed,
that he never got a double entendre
or complimented you on your "stems"?

If only you got to stay in Paris long enough
... to want to leave the party soon enough.

But perhaps that's all moot. Nothing hits home
until you've been gargoyle-d.
That you crooned, "I have a lover,"
as if you invented it, as if those
piggy-pigs never did exist.

                    Still, Miss Barracuda, Miss Angelfish,
Mrs. School of Dramatic Art:

I think of you often these days, and now,
of how you confuse the rose for
a manse, and find a world
in the haunted and twitching eye
of a violet brooch.

(The iron sharp and tang of ennui circulates
like so much drowsy blood.)

But that in the light fibulations of your black aigrette,
in the weight and peculiar double tone of
every satin swag, you manage your own dark
and aberrant materials, smile (flirt to the last),
as you don your nighttime wear in the daytime.

Charlotte Waking

First wild—
to stride out onto the world-historical stage,
a mind forming arcs and knives.

Yet that morning I asked myself only
what is red?

Perhaps a scent—
days fringed with wine-stain, sedition
heating the blood.

A moment of class self-discovery,
and a girl feeling singular.

Need and the broken reek of salt
brought me close
to a body furred with sickness and dazzle.

I saw myself in the bathwater, a question mark
and all animal elegance too.

Later I'm the despair of my sex,
or the ambivalence scored from a revolutionary act.
I'm lovely like a martyr, and just as disfigured.

The world drags itself along . . .
I try a hairdo à la Marat as an afterthought.

Antigone

My throat clears in the clean light of tragedy. The uncoiling blue of vultures in the wild spaces beyond the city seduces. Broken fingernails, a king's shame. And my brother, his death washes me open. *Je t'adore, brigand.* Ismene whispers and fidgets. Proper women hang themselves, day after day. But a cry of clarity shoots through the wrists, strong as a color. I have been waiting all my life. Raw peonies twist in the landscape, as the night sky licks its sleeves. The text? The text is corrupt.

They Say Women Are a Nuisance on Safari

We didn't get what we wanted.
We were solemn, we shook our names
off the pier, as ambitious as morning.
One thought she could eat her frailest child,
another that she could fly. Still another believed
her blush would heat the waters. We went
plucking nevertheless, slightly touched and
altogether clarified by the expedition.
Made tricky by ambiguity, we tasted young, and
like its general nature, we wouldn't stop. Oh bang
bang. We were punctual and figuratively that
sort of grace.

Year of the Gallows Birds

No ox in the breast, no ox on the person.
The snort is as false as the mind.
Let me be lucky and sooner, impervious
as I claw to be and to add.
In this bad, the rat clicks its heels,
casual and toothy. No dragons to
outmaneuver, how sorely missed they are.
A single bone, as if in anticipation of
a body, remembers the scabrous
curve of broken lust. The dog has its
way with the idle afternoon. So there
we are, in low relief: creaturely, comely,
deducible wholly by what we have lost.

You Could Feel That Freedom Coming On Too

Keep up your bright swords, for the dew will rust them.
— *Othello,* Shakespeare

———

The saddening ways slam
back and forth like a metal screendoor.
Delicious odors get through, as do
the latest pop songs and phrases
such as "no great shakes."
Facts are bigger now
though not necessarily more compelling.
Weather furnishes new romance:
it is lovely to see the natural world
hardly desert itself.
The soft terror of an untwisting bud
is no light thing. Even weak seasons
appear the opposite of bad logic.
After an entire day
of human custom (with its wrong
languages and funny temperatures),
a storm blades open.
(I think it feels itself alone.)
Swordlike in its skyplay,
but mainly loud, like an
Old Testament prophet,
it tears into your middle—
hollering its explosive intimacies
as a child would, or a hunger-bear
enjoying its own unreasonable
and indecent shapes.

All the Red Populations

What the influence of beast is
In my mass and canter? Sweet Cat, say.
Can't return to the white Sundays
Reiterated with rhododendrons and
Cold cream. Such gnawings on
The bone, standing up at the
Kitchen counter. Paprika? Tungsten?
A mettle whiff, my best worst deeds.
Cat, how you grow genuine.
                          What softest
Malice will clean from wraps and roots?
Cat Cat my Dog Cat, I stole your tread.
Beaded with wrong help, a cheek scarred
By rough salt. This poem is for us.
Your unkindness takes care of everything.
The stem strains at what we gather. Such
Privacy has a wild prettiness, a spice box
At its heart. It's the bright of true rot, a
Red ache for a braincase.
                          The odd quiddity,
Of you Cat, ringing my edges in cross stitch
And suture. Poor longhand journal, I'm leaving you.
A bit of milk, and we raise our faces—
I smell your longing, thinking
To snapping, (delighted!) in my pelt.

The Sea, The Sea

No, I've never had a real attraction to it, my worst fear is death by drowning.
Though I like some of the accessories: the conch shells, the clamdigger pants,
the salt in the hair. The faded look of shore houses. Someone is writing inside.
Punched-up town newsletter. Curios all sea-themed. I'm no swimmer. I fantasize
that at night, amidst the sleeping dogs and guttering candles, the sea prepares for
the worst. It rises and salts, ebbs and pools through everything. Not cleansing or
covering, but more as if that colossal blue makes for failings of a language it doesn't
itself speak. Shunts things about, while fish wait patiently. The water breaks, swells:
bone and a day dieted down to nothing. The sea is not small-minded, though at its
most breathtaking it's a *trompe l'oeil*. I'm a fool for watery adverbs. Disbelievingly. I
fear its sharks, lack of oxygen, sailor bric-a-brac, but at a distance I take pleasure in
its undulating order and disorder.

Just Disaster

Just Disaster

We stopped to watch the accident.
Fire! It had finally come to pass.
Just as surely as I was a coward
carrying a wolf. It stepped out from me,
it was paradise leaving me, running towards
the giant idea of that melting house.
So often you don't think,
"Little nicks of monstrosity, I shall be splendid in it."

Lucky Duck

Be large with those small fears. The whole sky
has fallen on you and all you can do about it is
shout, dragging your fear-ettes by their pinked ears.

They dance a number now: consequence without
sequence. Lovingly broadminded in their
realization and ruin, expert at the parting shot.

Not so small after all, we micro to
macro, swelling to the horror shows
lifted from the sly ways of life.

You, both scorched and shining in the terror
of the equivocal moment, its box of cheeky
logics rattling cold certainties out of bounds

and into the plaits of a girl's desirous ends.
A little debauched, the flirt in a freckling,
wondering spun to falling comes to this

pert contract of a paradox: saying things
because they will do no good, ringing change
in frumpy mono-determination, fruity and fruitless.

Exploded out of shelter, the tides come roaring in.
Let in the hoarse Cassandras and the dull pain of the
storyteller. You've needed those eyes all along.

We thought them disconcerting at first,
but it's the only way. You live here now
having exchanged etiquette for energy.

Don't be clever, don't be shy! Participate today.
Yesterday you say everything for their own sake,
and soon enough, tomorrow, you learn a lot from them.

There Is No Wing Like Meaning

All afternoon it's 1950s North American Method at the revival house: Brando, Clift, Monroe, and Dean. They appear to be saying, just imagine one has a soul. Intent on being expressive rather than lovely, they are practically breaking with light and dark.

Miss Bobby isn't hiding very much today. The drag queens in Marlena's are showing off the hard work of femininity. Some whisper too much along the lines of retaliatory self-invention, but still I can't deny the incandescence of such beautiful love letters. Pearl de la Cruz has taken the stage and her distances look supreme on her. She loves, insists Miss Bobby, to show off her revisions.

André Malraux spoke of his *Museum Without Walls* as a space where artworks would lose their properties as objects and gain their essences as style. David Antin writes: Somewhere in the image there is a proposition. Maria Callas once said, "I don't go out very much. I don't put myself on exhibit. I live in seclusion. I am wild. Very."

Wittgenstein writes: But the picture cannot place itself outside of its form of representation.

Dear unkind world, should we wonder after quiddity? I mean, I do, I can't help it. Chuang-tzu maintains that the utmost man uses the heart like a mirror. On the other hand, Akhmatova writes: For seventeen months I have been screaming.

In graduate school, I felt at once lustful and embarrassed in the presence of such relentless absences: the *mise en abîmes,* the doggy aporias, the hallucinatory effects of one thousand and one types of ambiguity. We traveled from land to landscape, to the interior of the exterior. Much of it was French, and much of it was *Fwench.*

Balanchine would say to his dancers, don't act, just do the steps. The steps will tell it like it really is. But a body will always walk away, leaving you in a wake of afterimages, artificial and true.

My friend Clem dates only magicians. According to her, they make a drama of the point where the possible intercepts the actual.

Erika, née Hector, also tells me that the irreconcilable is something grand. These rifts, these hungry expressibles, they are swiftly drawing me on.

"Wish You Were Here"

There is the ground between loving and being pleased. See, it is a city unto itself. Assess the points of entry, encampment, and escape. Level your eyes on the jagged horizon before your thoughts begin to scale. The mythological expressions that you feel coming on are merely exquisite irritations, curling routes that overrun the cityscape. The language never flies straight to the meaning, but in the meantime the sunsets here are quite resplendent.

Equilibrium

The ferocity of the world inside has the might of weeds.[1] If I could break hard enough to let it have its full expression, I could tell of the stabbing dawns and of how the trees were dreaming while I stood awake and watchful.

I remember the stupidity and feckless joy of eating an orange in front of the Orangerie. Language is all kink and stitch and funny bone.[2] And it is even funnier (barely answerable) proof that in circumstances which today would seem insufferable, you lived.

I feel so "personal" despite the fact that I am standing alongside myself, subject to dispersal. There is "freeplay," parataxis, dislocation, and ellipsis; and then there is the matter of "going to pieces."[3]

There comes a time when you stop wondering whether the phoenix rounding the corner is coming toward you or running away. You know only that a part of you is always holding a feather in your hand. Is this lyric resistance or a melancholy of the body?[4]

---

[1] ". . . the truthful precipitates of dreams, in which his taste for crime, his erotic obsessions, his savagery, his chimeras, his utopian sense of life and matter, even his cannibalism, pour out, on a level not counterfeit and illusory, but interior." (Antonin Artaud, *Theatre of Cruelty, First Manifesto*)

[2] "I come to terms with my materials. They know and I know that we're going to try something." (Robert Rauschenberg, *Rauschenberg*)

[3] "To go to pieces so pointlessly and unnecessarily." (Franz Kafka, *Diaries*)

[4] ". . . gesture which relates to the whole architectural space of the stage and has an effect like singing and gesture which relates to the dancer's own body and so has the effect of a spoken tone." (Edwin Denby, *Dance Writings and Poetry*)

I sing as a girl shedding the fever garden, as a boy tasting the knife of her.[5] Word-slung and feral, I happen upon "those places in the body that have no language"[6] but there really is no shielding in the end.

I am not thinking here of the model in which the body reproaches the mind. For miles, there is ceaseless verdure: you run through the bad woods of yourself every which way. Who can tell the forest for everything falling out of the trees? You keep on the run.[7]

Is it possible to escape psychology? You are both propelled and drained by it.[8] Much of the time you wander around like the hero in a classic noir picture, an amnesiac bounded by blackout.

Take away the mad lovelies and what's still left but the signature[9] force of you, and it moves upon a hundred legs.[10]

---

[5] "I showed this girl my stitches / She said she had some too / She said she thinks she'll start a rock band too." (Kristin Hersh, Throwing Muses, "Fall Down")

[6] Michel de Certeau, *The Practice of Everyday Life*

[7] "Their sober friendliness of manner can have, as Balanchine once wrote, an expression such as one imagines angels would have, who can take part in tragic events without becoming themselves miserable." (Edwin Denby, *Looking at the Dance*)

[8] ". . . the art of looking at ourselves as though we were characters in one of our novels . . . as the way to put ourselves in a position to think constructively and reap the benefits." (Cesare Pavese, *Journals*)

[9] "The fatal signature appear'd / To all the multitude, / Distinct as when the accursed pen / Had traced it with fresh blood." (Robert Southey, "All for Love")

[10] "Though I am speaking about sensibility only . . . these are grave matters." (Susan Sontag, "Notes on Camp")

Afraid I am come out softlypernicious, selfeating.[11]

You'd like something of maximum vehemence and physical grace. Instead, "A Day! Help! Help! Another Day!"[12]

"The wound is healed only by the spear that smote you."[13] ("You don't ask why in Wagner").[14]
and
" . . . no longer do you want this savagery. What you want instead is kindness."[15]

---

[11] "Who is to confirm for me the truth or probability of this, that it is only because of my literary mission that I am uninterested in all other things and therefore heartless." (Franz Kafka, *Diaries*)

[12] Emily Dickinson, 42

[13] Richard Wagner, *Parsifal*

[14] Lanford Wilson, *Burn This*

[15] Lesley Stern, *The Smoking Book*

After a Furious Fashion: Pairings

Shrimp chips and a tentative heart. (No, it's the mind that's strewing dissatisfaction like so many fall leaves.) Fluorescent lights and a shaky voice—so ugly it sounds like weeping and the word *faltering.* (Clackety phenomenon of speech.) Behold! and my generation. (Say the word, but can you point to something without the hooded eyes?) Rainfall and zestful self-pity. (Who can resist?) Bonnard's shy, dimpled nudes and your blurred abstraction. (Lassitude or Energy, which is the True Confession?)

Children keep growing like trees in the deep forests,
And fruit keeps its time as always.
Longing continues to find itself in the winds,
As dancers search and demonstrate without need of gain.
Streetlights, violence, and the sorcery of music
Play forever, despite every loneliness—
And you, you ask for an approach to all this.

An awkward word and a cluster of sweet pea:
This, to give the sense of cost, and
That, to stave off all such ridiculous charges.

Triply So

That dulled love.
        Soft and watched.

      Weak tea, that sort of violence.

O Lapse. Mend with sugar,
        a rosette in the mouth
  or two.

      Deck with the motion
of plummet,

          (there the twinge blooms fastest)

      errors snapping all the way.

A chin split,
      as she was sobbing
  and spitting.

      —Now have I done it? she asked,
        in spite.

That was the beginning
      of the new tooth.

        O strange grace:

One-legged, smelling of cedar,
housed in
blinking low-lights. She broods.

Mean heart: Dark minotaur.
Gentle cow,
horsey girl.

What remembers
you will yet
wish you back
into this world.

There, the
little clump of trees.
Wet evenings,
cold open

down. Your legs mottled
with the chill,
tender at inevitable.

The geese pulling
overhead,
having nothing   nothing
to do with you.

Touring, Touring, Gone

Seneca writes: Consider it a great thing to play the part of one single man.

———

I carrot them with caramels,
and the bedlam of tuba and tambourine.
I hang the air with barbeque smoke
winding up my walk and my weft.
I longitude, I latitude, I spangle
from the core.
                    Ricochet my way
to the eavesdrop—will they come at all?
A dragon skin of oriental chromas
rests at the foot of their pout and shrug.
I lob rare desert flora in their traffic-stopper's
palms, cut roses from arterial tissue.
The afternoon tap runs unheeded.
I mise-en-scène, then puppeteer. I perfect
my gargouillades.
                    They finally approach
with haggard dawn and cabaret smiles.
I hum a tired bit at first. Wild a little.
They burn uneven tones.
I twang in the pending abracadabra.
Come harry this. Sardonic and
auroral too, their time will crest,
will hasp. They goad me in the rushes:
(I monkey, I orangutan,)
leonine, hexed, come catch them—

Afterword

There is no doubt that their encasements cast a spell on our young heroine. *Dahlias, molto adagio, pedestrian.* Monsieur Pépé Le Pew recounts how he once sent her a *french kiss* as a going away present. *Dark meat.* Her description in *Cross Words and Other Stories* shows that she imagined the package to resemble an intricate European pastry. *Wolf whistle, thicket.* Enchantment was its own little summa.

The contexts were various: in potboilers, in medical journals, out of the mouths of elevator folk, bringing the world into her room, bestrewing the nightstand as the words shed their layers—by turns pinprick precise, woolly, or unquietly resonant. Burning sometimes. *Epaulettes, tourism, tipple, bark.* Shape over shape, they could open and close like fists. And in the cone of light thrown by her childhood lamp, they seemed to be shards of color, in a dancehall full of mirrors. *Infra, provenance, indeed, Bela Lugosi.*

Much later, what emerged unexpectedly but *poppy.* Nodding red, nodding orange, but always darkly nodding away. Between her and poppy, a torn-up world of cause and effect, pasts and prologues, broken clocks, the clatter in parting.

Sailor, Your Sonnet

now i forget home.
trade seasonal myths for the seasons.
where an inner life should be, a leaf-proud exterior is carrying on.
been cut to be the high prow for a ship.
wake and feel the fell of nothing.
i am a vehicle in the water.
dusk. cloud.
for example, human love.
now i've never wanted anything.
nights flock like birds.
you've nailed to me, the most improbable things.
these things reprise in the collective dreaming.
for example, the sailor died alone, going westward.
in a dry season, they've dipped me gently into the sea.

Full Sail and Trembling

This fucking world—
torrential rain, small talk
filling up the room.

Blind Future

Beautiful crewmate, beware
the wild grasses on the other shore.
What's most frightening is that
they almost didn't happen too.
And the indifference of the island
bellows from shelf to shelf. A turtle rubs along.
The old volcanoes have seen everything,
and their kind, flat expressions seem almost
like a snub. The ancient rains maybe think on us.
—We hope even that much.
The place has its own absurdities moreover:
a soufflé falls in the night, the lone botanist
plants dark red poetry in the reefs.
And the pains of work and love? Oh yes,
how dare we suppose they don't inhabit
the very splendor of the landscape.
—Now the wind stops at nothing.
And once upon land:
a verdant arena of second thoughts
grew where I grew. And you, you were scalded
awake by the dappling on the waters.
This is how we came to be on yet another sea,
persuaded of its strangest harbors.
And each time the arrivals interest me less,
each time I find I murmur, *so this is the sea.*

Acknowledgments

Grateful acknowledgment is made to the editors of the following journals in which these poems first appeared: *American Letters & Commentary*, "Ballad of the Last Chance"; *Boston Review*, "A Village Journal"; *Colorado Review*, "After a Furious Fashion: Pairings," "The Horse and Its Rider"; *Denver Quarterly*, "Equilibrium"; *Good Foot*, "In Radiant Serenity"; *Gulf Coast*, "Loveliest Grotesque"; *Indiana Review*, "Where Metaphorical Moves Get Started," "The Red Smile"; *MARGIE*, "Vexed Pressed Frock"; *ZYZZYVA*, "Something Something Something Grand."

Deepest gratitude to my wonderful teachers for their inspiration and guidance. Love to my family and friends for their support, patience, and encouragement along the way. Thanks to the MacDowell Colony for time to edit this manuscript. And special thanks to Marilyn Chin and all the good people at Kore Press.